World Black History

The Slave Trade

Melody Herr

Heinemann
LIBRARY

www.heinemannlibrary.co.uk
Visit our website to find out more information about Heinemann Library books.

To order:

☎ Phone +44 (0) 1865 888066

🖷 Fax +44 (0) 1865 314091

🖳 Visit www.heinemannlibrary.co.uk

Heinemann Library is an imprint of Capstone Global Library Limited, a company incorporated in England and Wales having its registered office at 7 Pilgrim Street, London, EC4V 6LB – Registered company number: 6695582

"Heinemann" is a registered trademark of Pearson Education Limited, under licence to Capstone Global Library Limited

Text © Capstone Global Library Limited 2010
First published in hardback in 2010
The moral rights of the proprietor have been asserted.

Edited by David Andrews, Louise Galpine, and Abby Colich
Designed by Ryan Frieson and Betsy Wernert
Illustrated by Mapping Specialists
Picture research by Mica Brancic
Originated by Heinemann Library
Printed by China Translation and Printing Services Ltd

ISBN 978 0 431194 02 8 (hardback)
14 13 12 11 10
10 9 8 7 6 5 4 3 2 1

British Library Cataloguing in Publication Data
Herr, Melody
The slave trade. – (World black history)
909'.0496-dc22
A full catalogue record for this book is available from the British Library.

Acknowledgements

We would like to thank the following for permission to reproduce photographs: ©AKG-images p. **39**; ©Alamy pp. **11** (North Wind Picture Archives), **16** (Classic Image), **18** (The Print Collector), **20** (The Print Collector), **15** (Lordprice Collection), **24** (Mary Evans Picture Library); ©The Art Archive p. **27** (Gianni Dagli Orti); ©The Bridgeman Art Library pp. **6** (John Martin), **37**, **41**, **43** (Christie's Images/Private Collection); ©British Library p. **21**; ©Corbis pp. **4** (epa/©Nic Bothma), **8** (Stapleton Collection/Historical Picture Library/Philip Spruyt), **13** (Bettmann), **23** (Hemis/©Philippe Body), **19** (Cordaiy Photo Library Ltd./©Colin Hoskins), **25** (Stapleton Collection/Historical Picture Library), **28** (Bettmann), **35** (Stapleton Collection/Historical Picture Library), **36** (Bettmann), **38**; ©Getty Images pp. **7** (Time Life Pictures/Photo by Eliot Elisofon), **10** (Hulton Archive), **22** (MPI), **31** (Mansell/Time Life Pictures), **32** (Hulton Archive), **33** (Hulton Archive/Stringer), **34** (Rischgitz), **42** (Hulton Archive); ©North Wind Picture Archives pp. **26**, **30**; ©Scala, Florence p. **14** (HIP 2009).

Cover photograph of the deck of the captured slave-ship *Wildfire* brought into Key West, USA, in 1860 reproduced with permission of North Wind/© North Wind Picture Archives.

We would like to thank Marika Sherwood and Stephanie Davenport for their invaluable help in the preparation of this book.

Disclaimer

All the Internet addresses (URLs) given in this book were valid at the time of going to press. However, due to the dynamic nature of the Internet, some addresses may have changed, or sites may have changed or ceased to exist since publication. While the author and Publishers regret any inconvenience this may cause readers, no responsibility for any such changes can be accepted by either the author or the Publishers.

Contents

Some words are shown in bold, **like this**. You can find out what they mean by looking in the Glossary.

Africa in the 1400s

Africa in the 1400s was a rich, diverse land. The Songhay people were building West Africa's greatest empire, in the land where the Mali people once reigned. In central Africa, kings in the Congo and Benin ruled powerful nations. In the east, **merchants** in cities along the coast shipped goods to Asia and Arabia. Regular taxation, **toll** collection on trade routes, and systems of government existed in many kingdoms and empires.

A time of change

But a time of change was beginning. Around 1440 European traders came to West Africa. At first they wanted to buy ivory and gold. But soon they wanted to buy workers, and some Africans were willing to sell **prisoners of war** to the traders. Over the next 420 years, this trade in human beings – the slave trade – changed African societies and the lives of millions of people forever.

The kingdom of Songhay

The kingdom of Songhay was the last of the great West African kingdoms, following the kingdoms of Ghana and Mali. It was also the largest, stretching across much of West Africa.

This kingdom was a centre of trade. Salt and gold from nearby mines were often traded. The city of Timbuktu, on the Niger River, was a centre of learning. People came from as far away as India to study philosophy and science in the university.

This mosque (Islamic place of worship) was built in West Africa.

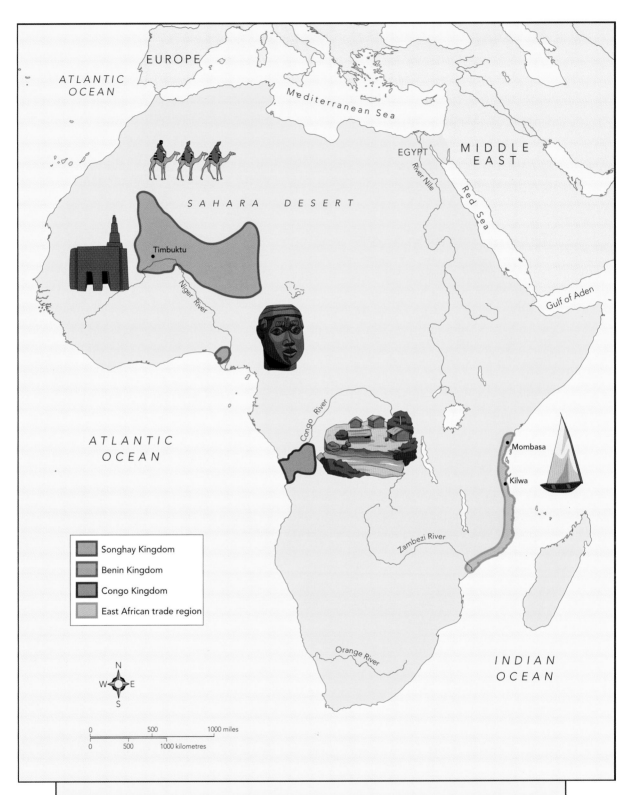

EUROPE

ATLANTIC
OCEAN

Mediterranean Sea

MIDDLE
EAST

EGYPT

River Nile

Red Sea

Gulf of Aden

SAHARA   DESERT

Timbuktu

Niger River

ATLANTIC
OCEAN

Congo River

Mombasa

Kilwa

Zambezi River

Songhay Kingdom

Benin Kingdom

Congo Kingdom

East African trade region

N
W   E
S

| 0 | 500 | 1000 miles |
| 0 | 500 | 1000 kilometres |

Orange River

INDIAN
OCEAN

This map shows just some of the societies thriving in Africa in the 1400s.
Tall mosques rose up in Songhay. Metalworkers crafted bronze sculptures in
Benin, and busy villages thrived in the Congo. Merchants traded in the East.

Newcomers from Europe

Africa was a place to buy ivory, peppers, copper, silver, and gold. Africans had sold these luxuries to traders from the Mediterranean, the **Middle East**, and Asia for hundreds of years. Then, in 1443, a new group of traders arrived. They came from Portugal, a small nation in western Europe. Over the next 60 years, they explored the west coast of Africa, rounded the southern tip, and sailed up the east coast.

Traders in East Africa

In East Africa, the Portuguese found thriving cities along the coast. Ships came in and out of their harbours, trading gold and ivory with the Middle East and Asia. Here is how one newcomer described Kilwa, the most famous of these cities:

> The city comes down to the shore, and is entirely surrounded by a wall and towers, within which there are may be 12,000 inhabitants. The country all round is very luxurious with many trees and gardens of all sorts of vegetables, citrons, lemons, and the best sweet oranges that were ever seen.

This map shows the East African coastline in the 1500s. Many thriving cities of trade existed along this coast.

The Portuguese built forts to protect their new trading posts along the coast of East Africa.

Unwelcome visitors

East African and Arab traders didn't welcome the newcomers. In response, the Portuguese attacked the coastal cities. They built forts to defend their new trading posts. In this way, they managed to take a share of the business.

Traders in West Africa

In West Africa, however, traders welcomed the Portuguese. The ruler of the Congo, for example, allowed them to trade with the citizens of his kingdom. Eventually this business relationship became friendship. The Congo king invited **missionaries** to his court. He converted to Christianity. He also adopted European-style clothing, manners, and laws. He sent young men to study in schools in Portugal.

The Portuguese co-operated with other West African traders as well. Ship captains agreed to haul goods up and down the Atlantic coast from one African trading post to another. In exchange for cloth, metal tools, and other European goods, the Portuguese received copper, ivory, and gold.

An age of exploration

The Portuguese came to Africa during Europe's age of exploration. They were not only interested in trading with the Africans. They were also searching for a route to Asia, where they could find expensive goods such as silk and spices. Some explorers tried to reach Asia by sailing around Africa. In 1498 Vasco da Gama proved that this route was possible, although it was also long and dangerous.

Meanwhile, Christopher Columbus tried sailing west. In 1492, with ships given to him by the king and queen of Spain, he sailed across the Atlantic Ocean until he reached land. He thought he had arrived in Asia. In fact, he had stumbled into the Americas.

This discovery would have a huge impact on Africa. Before Europeans settled in the Americas, the Portuguese would sometimes buy enslaved Africans from African traders. But with so much work to be done in this new land, slaves were in higher demand than ever before.

Christopher Columbus landed in America in 1492.

European colonies in the Americas

Spain started **colonies** on the Caribbean islands soon after Columbus' first voyage. A colony was a place where a European nation sent settlers to build new towns. Colonists also grew crops and found and produced riches for their home nation. While **conquistadors** searched for gold, colonists planted sugar cane. Sugar was a luxury in Europe, and sugar cane grew well in the Caribbean climate.

Portugal soon started colonies as well. In the early 1500s, Portuguese settlers colonised Brazil, in South America, where they mined gold and grew sugar cane.

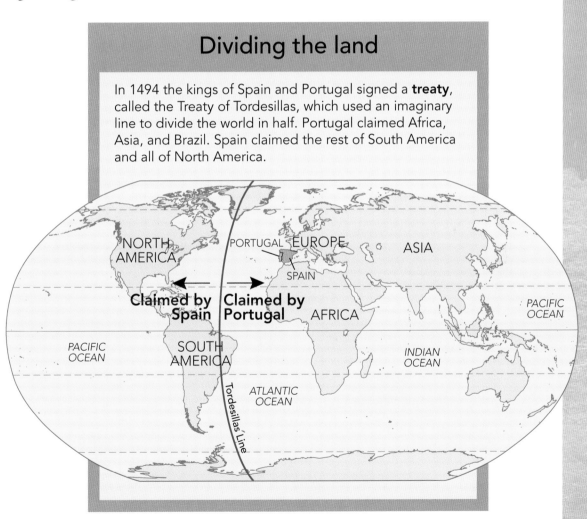

Dividing the land

In 1494 the kings of Spain and Portugal signed a **treaty**, called the Treaty of Tordesillas, which used an imaginary line to divide the world in half. Portugal claimed Africa, Asia, and Brazil. Spain claimed the rest of South America and all of North America.

Workers wanted

The colonists couldn't work the mines and the sugar cane plantations by themselves. At first the colonists tried to force people native to the Americas to work. But thousands died from **smallpox**, measles, and other European diseases. Those who survived resisted the colonists. Some fled from the colonies. When the colonists realised that they couldn't rely on native workers, they decided to buy slaves.

Slavery

Slavery meant one person – the owner – could treat another person – the slave – as property. Slaves didn't choose to be slaves. They became slaves either because their parents were slaves or because they were captured and sold.

Every day, every hour of their lives, slaves had to obey their owners completely. Slaves received no pay for their work. Everything, including their clothes, their food, and even their children, belonged to their owners. Slaves had no rights and could be tortured and beaten by their owners. Slaves were not even considered human beings.

This master whips an enslaved African whose hands and feet are bound together.

African slaves

Since the 1440s, European traders had sometimes bought slaves from Africans who were willing to enslave and sell their enemies. So when the colonists wanted slaves, traders went to Africa to get them. In 1518 traders took the first shipment of enslaved Africans directly from Africa to the colonies in the Americas. This terrible event marked the beginning of the slave trade across the Atlantic Ocean. This trade in human beings would last more than 400 years, and it would enslave more than 12 million Africans.

A black explorer

One of the first explorers of southern and western North America was an enslaved African. Estevanico was the slave of a Spanish conquistador. In a journey that lasted from 1528 to 1536, the explorers travelled hundreds of kilometres, through what is now the western United States and Mexico. They survived shipwreck, disease, and hunger. They were captured by some Native Americans along the way and made friends with others. Hundreds of men started the journey, but only Estevanico and three others lived to tell the tale.

This illustration shows explorers crossing from what is now Texas, USA, into Mexico in the early 1500s.

Colonies and slaves

Portugal and Spain grew wealthy from their new **colonies**. Soon other European rulers sent explorers to claim land in the Americas. Over the next 150 years, the Dutch and the French colonised areas of North and South America. On the Caribbean islands, colonists started sugar plantations and imported enslaved African workers.

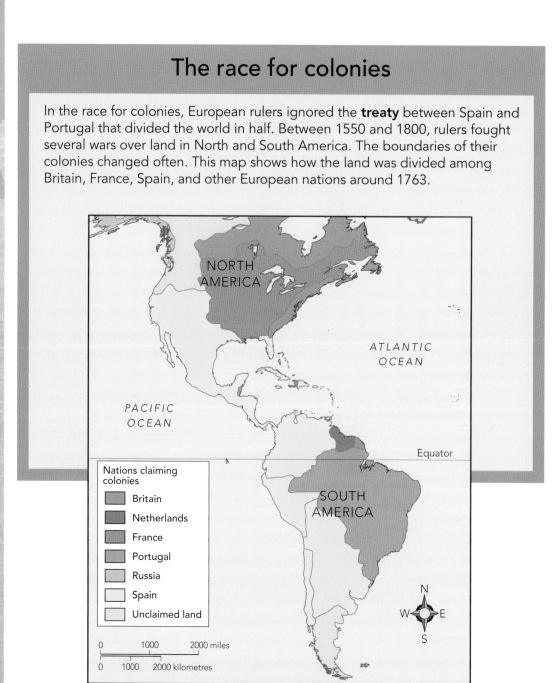

The race for colonies

In the race for colonies, European rulers ignored the **treaty** between Spain and Portugal that divided the world in half. Between 1550 and 1800, rulers fought several wars over land in North and South America. The boundaries of their colonies changed often. This map shows how the land was divided among Britain, France, Spain, and other European nations around 1763.

NORTH AMERICA

ATLANTIC OCEAN

PACIFIC OCEAN

Equator

SOUTH AMERICA

Nations claiming colonies

- Britain
- Netherlands
- France
- Portugal
- Russia
- Spain
- Unclaimed land

0   1000   2000 miles

0   1000   2000 kilometres

N
W · E
S

British colonies in the Caribbean

Britain, too, joined the race for colonies. Colonists tried to grow several different crops on the Caribbean islands, but after a few years they switched to sugar cane. Following the lead of their European neighbours, they too imported enslaved Africans to work the sugar plantations.

British colonies in North America

Britain also began to establish colonies along the Atlantic coast of North America. In 1607 the first settlers arrived in the area that later became Virginia. They were sponsored by a group of London businessmen. They named their colony Jamestown, after King James I.

Only 12 years later, in 1619, the first Africans were brought to Jamestown. The sea captain who sold them to the colonists had probably thought of the Africans as slaves. The colonists who bought them, however, treated them as **indentured servants**. After the Africans worked for a few years, their buyers allowed them to go free.

The first Africans arrived in Jamestown in 1619.

Servants as workers

Buying workers from Europe and setting them free was common during this time. These workers were called indentured servants. They were usually young working-class men, although older people and women were sometimes indentured. A servant agreed to work four to seven years in return for passage to America. After the agreed period of time, he or she was a free person.

More workers needed

Soon, though, there were not enough indentured servants. The supply couldn't keep up with the demand for workers in Virginia, Massachusetts, South Carolina, and other new British colonies. Southern colonists, in particular, needed labourers on tobacco and rice plantations. Yet fewer British citizens wanted to work as servants. So between 1600 and 1750, British colonists began turning to slavery as the answer to the worker shortage.

Labourers were needed to work on tobacco plantations.

Making sugar

Sugar cane, a tall plant similar to corn, grew well in the hot, wet climate of Brazil and the Caribbean islands. From the 1500s to the 1800s, slaves did most of the work on the sugar plantations.

Slaves first planted the young stalks in the fields. When the crop was ready, they used machetes, or long knives, to cut down the thick canes. They loaded the canes on carts and hauled them to the mill for the first step of the sugar-making process.

At the mill, a huge machine crushed and ground the canes to squeeze out the juice. Slaves collected this sweet juice and took it to the boiling house. There they boiled the juice for several hours until the water evaporated and only the brown grains of raw sugar were left. After the sugar cooled, slaves weighed it and packed it into barrels.

These slaves cut down sugar cane in the Caribbean in the 1800s.

European slave traders

In the 1500s, the slave trade was a small business, involving a few ships and a few thousand slaves. As the demand for slaves rose during the 1600s and 1700s, the slave trade grew into a huge, international **enterprise**. It became a business that involved kings and queens, traders, bankers, insurers, and millions of enslaved Africans.

Competing for profit

Europeans competed for the profits of the slave trade. The Portuguese, who had controlled trade with Africa in the 1500s, kept their forts in East Africa. But by 1700, the British, Dutch, and French controlled the slave trade from the West African coast.

Many European rulers supported the slave trade. In 1672, for example, a group of British businessmen formed the Royal African Company. They received a **charter** from King Charles II granting them the right to do business along the west coast of Africa. Eventually the king opened African trade to all **merchants**.

Sir John Hawkins

Sir John Hawkins made the first British slave voyage between Africa and the Americas in 1542. Queen Elizabeth I encouraged the slave trade and loaned Hawkins one of her own ships.

Royal business

British rulers supported the slave trade because they collected huge taxes from it. It also provided jobs for captains and sailors, ship builders and dockworkers, farmers and factory workers. It also helped create a transport system connecting Britain and its **colonies**.

The trade triangle

A sea captain for the Royal African Company sailed a triangle-shaped route, linking Britain, Africa, and the Americas. On each part of the voyage, he carried goods produced in one place to buyers in another place.

A captain started the triangular route in Britain. He loaded his ship with cloth, tools, guns, metal bars, jewellery, and other factory-made items. Then he sailed to a port on the west coast of Africa, where he exchanged these goods for enslaved men, women, and children.

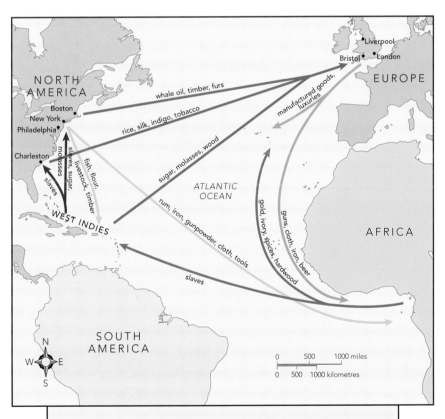

The triangle-shaped slave trade route connected Europe, Africa, and the Americas.

Slaves loaded sugar for shipment to Europe.

To the colonies and home

After trading goods for slaves in Africa, the captain sailed across the Atlantic Ocean to the Americas. He sold the slaves in the colonies, and he reloaded his ship with sugar, tobacco, rice, **indigo**, and other natural products that he could sell to factory owners back home.

Finally, he crossed the Atlantic again and returned to Britain. There, he sold his **cargo**, bought another shipment of factory-made goods, and set out for Africa to sail the triangle once again.

Europeans in Africa

Africa was an important part of the trade triangle, but Europeans considered Africa a deadly place. Every year, traders and sailors died from **yellow fever**, **malaria**, and other tropical diseases. Europeans seldom went beyond the coast for another reason: powerful African rulers didn't welcome outsiders. Europeans were only allowed to build a few trading posts along the coast.

Justifying slavery?

Europeans had many ways of trying to justify enslaving Africans. Colonists claimed Africans could tolerate the hot climate better than Europeans could. They also claimed it was their duty to convert Africans to Christianity and to "**civilize**" them.

Slave owners told themselves that Africans were not equal to Europeans. Even important scholars claimed that Africans were less intelligent, less sensitive, and even less human than Europeans. Therefore, Europeans insisted that they should be masters and Africans should be slaves.

For hundreds of years, prejudiced men and women ignored Africans' many achievements. **Racism** – the mistaken idea that a person's skin colour determines his or her value as a human being – is a long-lasting result of the slave trade.

Africans built the city of Great Zimbabwe between 1200 and 1450. For many years, though, archaeologists who were prejudiced against Africans wanted to believe that it had been built by other ancient people who settled in Africa. Today, tourists come to Great Zimbabwe to see one of Africa's many achievements.

African rulers and slave traders

In Africa, Europeans and Africans built a slave-trade network that covered central and West Africa. After they were captured, the enslaved Africans were marched from their homes to the nearest port along the coast.

Rules of the slave trade

European traders had to follow African rulers' laws. When Europeans wanted to build a trading post, they needed permission. Some rulers welcomed traders from any nation. Others made agreements with only one group. An African ruler could charge Europeans for trading rights or make them agree to purchase a certain number of slaves at a certain price. A ruler also expected money and gifts from time to time. In addition, Europeans had to pay taxes on the goods they bought and sold.

Slave traders used different types of money such as cowrie shells (below), brass or copper bracelets, and metal bars.

Gathering slaves

Africans collected slaves for European traders in many ways. A ruler could demand slaves as **tribute** from less powerful leaders or conquered neighbours. Enemies captured during a war could be enslaved. A person who committed a serious crime might be sentenced to slavery.

Searching for more slaves

As the price of slaves rose, African rulers and traders looked for ways to collect more slaves. Rulers sentenced more criminals to slavery and increased the number of slaves demanded as tribute. Traders raided villages or kidnapped villagers working in their fields.

Ayuba Suleiman Diallo

Slave traders might capture anyone – even another slave trader. For example, Ayuba Suleiman Diallo (who also used the name Job ben Solomon) was an educated Muslim **merchant** in West Africa. In 1730, immediately after selling slaves, he was captured, sold to a British slaver, and sent to a tobacco plantation in Maryland. Eventually he became free and returned to Africa in 1734.

Slaves and guns

Some African rulers supported the slave trade because it was a profitable business. In exchange for slaves, they purchased luxuries from around the world: silk, linen, jewellery, sugar, rum, and tobacco. They also bought useful items such as iron, copper, and tools.

What African rulers wanted most were guns, both to attack their enemies and to protect their own people. European slave traders not only sold the guns, but they also encouraged fighting among African nations so that they could buy the **prisoners of war**.

Working for the slave trade

Rulers and traders weren't the only Africans who profited from the slave trade. Interpreters helped Europeans bargain for slaves. Farmers sold their crops to ship captains to feed slaves. Boatmen rowed slaves to the ships. In one way or another, the slave trade had an effect on everyone in African society.

Slavery in Africa

Africans accepted the slave trade partly because slavery was not new to them. In Africa, as in Europe, some societies permitted slavery, but in general theirs was a more humane kind of slavery that respected human beings.

Slaves belonged to a separate **class**. A person could be a slave simply because his or her parents were slaves. Other people were enslaved because they were prisoners of war.

While some slaves in Africa were field hands or servants, others were soldiers or government officials. Sometimes slaves married their owners and became part of the family.

Pyramid builders

The biggest pyramid at Giza in Egypt is 230 metres (755 feet) tall. Who built it? Some historians say that Egyptian pharaohs used gangs of slaves to build the great pyramids. Others claim that free citizens built the pyramids during the months when they didn't have to work in the fields.

These pyramids at Giza may have been built by slaves.

Early slave trade

Buying and selling slaves had been taking place in Africa for generations. For centuries, merchants who crossed the Sahara Desert to trade in West Africa purchased small numbers of slaves. So did Arab merchants along the coast of East Africa.

The slave trade grows

When Europeans began to purchase enslaved Africans, however, they introduced a new kind of slavery. This new slave trade was much larger in scale. It stretched from the heartland of Africa to the **colonies** of the Americas and the cities of Europe. It also involved more businesspeople, from companies with royal **charters** to independent traders. Most importantly, it enslaved millions more African men, women, and children.

King Afonso I

Afonso I ruled Congo from 1506 to 1543. He was friendly towards the Portuguese traders. He also welcomed Portuguese craftspeople and **missionaries** to his court. In fact, "Afonso" wasn't the king's original African name. He adopted this European name when he converted to Christianity.

At first, slave traders in the Congo purchased prisoners of war. But as the demand for slaves in the colonies rose, traders began to kidnap the free people of the Congo. In 1526 Afonso sent a letter to King Joao II of Portugal. In the letter Afonso said that every day more and more of his people were being kidnapped, enslaved, and sold to Portuguese traders. Even the royal family wasn't safe.

The Tree of Forgetfulness

The kings of Dahomey, a kingdom in West Africa, sold thousands of Africans to slave traders. The kings made the slaves walk in circles around the "Tree of Forgetfulness" so that their spirits would not remember the terrible things they suffered and come back to curse the kings.

The kings of Dahomey sold fellow Africans to slave traders.

A different kind of slavery

Under this new kind of slavery, enslaved Africans were treated differently. Africans thought of the people sold into slavery as enemies or social outcasts. European traders thought of the enslaved as trade goods, while colonists in the Americas thought of them as work animals. According to the law, slaves were property; they had no legal rights. They were completely at the mercy of their owners, who could do with them as they liked. Once a person became a slave, he or she was usually a slave for the rest of his or her life. All of the enslaved's children were slaves, too.

The long journey

Africans who were caught in the terrible net of the slave trade from the late 1600s to the mid-1800s made a long journey across Africa, across the Atlantic Ocean, and into a life of slavery. It was a journey into misery, sickness, and fear. For several thousand, it was a journey into death.

> Slaves were forced to march to the coast.

March to the sea

After slaves were kidnapped from their village or captured during a war, a trader gathered them for the march to the coast. Depending on how far they had to travel, the march could last a few days or a few months. During the day, the captives walked in single file, tied to each other with ropes or chains. At night, they slept on the ground. They had no blankets; sometimes they had no clothing either. They were never given enough food. Under these conditions, many became ill and many died.

On the coast

When slaves reached a trading post on the coast, they were allowed to eat and bathe. Many still died. They were kept in prisons that were often overcrowded, with very little air or light, and no toilets. European buyers examined the slaves, chose the ones they wanted, and bargained over the price.

Slave "castles"

If a ship was ready, the slaves were put on board. If not, they were locked in a slave "castle", which was actually a dungeon-like prison. If the trading post didn't have a building for the slaves, they were forced to stay in a pen without a roof. Slaves sometimes waited as long as a year before a ship came.

Elmina "Castle"

Elmina "Castle", built by Portuguese traders in 1482, was the first centre for the Atlantic slave trade. European officials and their guests lived upstairs, while enslaved Africans were crowded into the stinking, dirty dungeons below.

Traders bought enslaved Africans at Elmina.

Slave ships

When a ship came, the slaves were taken from their prisons and put on board. In the 1700s, slave ships were like other **cargo** ships. They were built of wood, and they had huge sails because they relied on wind power. Ships came in many different sizes, ranging from 15 to 38 metres (50 to 125 feet) long and from 2.4 to 4.6 metres (8 to 15 feet) wide. Below the top deck, a ship had a set of lower decks, like shelves, for the human cargo.

Human cargo

The captain and **crew** thought of slaves as cargo. The more slaves the ship carried, the more profitable the voyage would be. When a ship reached Africa, carpenters built extra platforms between the decks in order to pack in more slaves.

Sailing ships transported slaves from West Africa to the **colonies** in the Americas.

How many slaves in a ship?

How many slaves a ship carried depended on its size. Small ships carried fewer than 100 slaves. Large ships carried more than 1,000. This drawing shows how slaves were packed on the ship *Brookes*.

Packing slaves

On the ship, enslaved men and women were separated from each other. There were always far more men, perhaps as many as two men for one woman, because they were sold for higher prices. But men were more likely to escape or rebel, so ship captains took extra steps to control them. The crew shackled the men in pairs and took them to the lower decks. There, they were chained to the floor, side by side, without enough space to sit up or roll over.

Enslaved women

Women were taken to a different part of the ship. Sometimes they were kept in cabins. Sometimes they were allowed to move around on the ship in order to cook and do other chores. If the ship was carrying children, they stayed with the women.

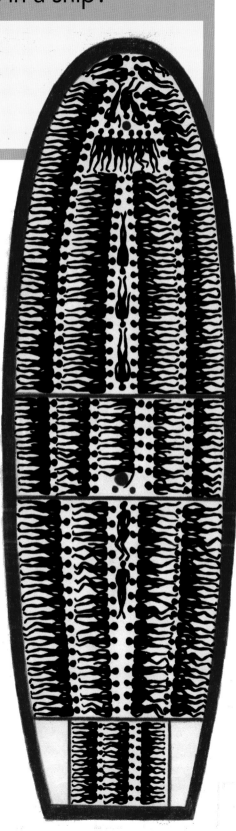

The Middle Passage

All this time, the enslaved Africans didn't know where they were going. In fact, they were about to begin the worst part of their journey: the **Middle Passage**. The Middle Passage was the 6,437-kilometre (4,000-mile) voyage across the Atlantic Ocean, from Africa to the colonies in the Americas.

Life on the ship

When the weather was good, the crew took the slaves to the top deck for fresh air and exercise. On stormy days, they had to stay in the dark, dirty hold. Slaves received two or three meals each day. They ate soup or mush made from beans, rice, yams, maize, and occasionally meat.

Usually the voyage lasted 50 to 80 days. But sailing ships depended on wind power. If the wind didn't blow strongly enough in the right direction, the voyage lasted twice as long. Then supplies ran low, and slaves weren't allowed much food or water.

Slavers jammed as many slaves as possible onto a ship in order to make the most profit.

Slaves were kept in cramped, dirty conditions on slave ships, where they were exposed to many diseases.

Disease and danger

Slaves suffered from **malaria**, **yellow fever**, **smallpox**, and diarrhoea. Diseases spread quickly because the slaves were packed so tightly and because the only toilet in the holds was a bucket. Although the crew occasionally cleaned the hold, it was a filthy, smelly place. In addition to diseases, slaves suffered from sores caused by shackles and chains.

Storms and pirates added to the dangers. During a shipwreck or an attack, the captain and crew were more likely to look out for themselves than to rescue the slaves.

Death

As a result of disease and other dangers, approximately 10 to 20 per cent of the slaves who left Africa died before they reached the colonies in the Americas. Their bodies were thrown into the ocean.

The *Leusden*

When the slave ship *Leusden* wrecked in 1738, the crew raced for the lifeboats, leaving the slaves chained to the lower decks of the sinking ship. The *Leusden* had sailed from Africa with 716 slaves; only 14 of them survived.

Making a profit

Why didn't the captain treat the slaves better? The purpose of the Middle Passage, like the rest of the slave trade, was to make a profit. In his view, slaves were cargo – not human beings. Slaves could be purchased cheaply in Africa and then sold for more money in the Americas. Therefore, the captain could make a profit even if many slaves died during the voyage.

Cruel treatment

Throughout the voyage, slaves were kept in shackles to prevent them from escaping or revolting. If they disobeyed orders, they were whipped. If they refused to eat, they were force-fed. Female slaves were sometimes abused by the captain and crew.

Healthy slaves brought high prices, but sick or dead slaves were worth nothing. When disease struck, the captain might order his crew to throw sick slaves overboard in an effort to prevent the disease from spreading. In 1781, for example, the captain of the slave ship *Zong* threw 133 sick slaves overboard.

When a slave died, the crew threw his or her body into the ocean. Sometimes they threw sick slaves overboard, too.

The Journey's End

When the ship landed at a port in the Americas, the slaves were given fresh food and allowed to bathe. Then they were sold to the buyers who offered the highest prices. Slaves were **branded** before being taken away by their new owners.

In North America, slaves worked in tobacco and cotton fields.

Slaves' work

Slaves taken to sugar plantations in the Caribbean or South America had short, hard lives. During the eight-month harvest season, they worked around the clock. Owners didn't provide enough food or good housing. Many slaves were killed in accidents or died from overwork after only a few years.

Slaves taken to North America lived longer, healthier lives because of a better climate and easier working conditions. But their lives were still hard.

Many jobs for slaves

Slaves did many different kinds of work for their owners. On the plantations, most of the slaves grew sugar cane, tobacco, **indigo**, rice, or cotton. A few were trained as carpenters or blacksmiths. Some worked as household servants.

Protest and resistance

The slave trade brought war, hardship, and insecurity to Africa. Some rulers spoke out against it and tried to keep their own people safe from traders. At the same time, enslaved Africans struggled for freedom.

Cost of the slave trade

Between 1500 and 1870, millions of Africans were enslaved. Most of them were young men, which meant that African societies lost many of the best farmers, hunters, builders, and workers. Families lost fathers, brothers, uncles, and sons. Those who were left had to find a way to keep their communities running. At the same time, they had to watch out for kidnappers and enemy warriors. As the slave trade spread across Africa, it brought grief and fear.

Slave raids, such as this one in Central Africa, tore apart families and communities.

African rulers protest

As African rulers watched the slave trade destroy their kingdoms, they began to protest. Some tried to outlaw the slave trade in their kingdoms, but traders simply went somewhere else. Other rulers insisted that traders obey certain laws. In the 1600s, for example, Queen Njinga of Ndongo sold war captives to Europeans. Yet she protected runaways whom she felt shouldn't have been enslaved, and she wouldn't allow traders to take her own people.

Protecting the people

Leaders tried to protect their people in other ways. King Tanja Musa, for example, built a wall around his city in western Africa. The slave raiders, however, still captured the people who had to go outside the city wall to farm, gather firewood, and fetch water. So the king built a second, larger wall around the fields.

Queen Njinga of Ndongo made rules for the slave trade in her territory.

Slave ship rebellions

Many enslaved Africans tried to fight for their freedom. During the **Middle Passage**, slaves sometimes tried to take over their ship. In 1769, for example, slaves on the ship *Guineese Vriendschap* rebelled. But the **crew** won the battle, put the slaves back in chains, and took them to the Americas where they were sold.

Rebellion in the colonies

In the **colonies**, plantation owners tried to prevent **rebellion** by punishing slaves when they disobeyed orders. Slaves still resisted. In 1739, nearly 100 slaves in Stono, South Carolina, started marching towards Florida, where they hoped to be free. Colonists quickly recaptured and executed them. Although the Stono Rebellion failed, it showed that slaves would risk their lives for freedom.

The *Guineese Vriendschap*

Essjerrie Ettin led a slave rebellion on the Dutch slave ship, the *Guineese Vriendschap* in 1769. They nearly succeeded, but a nearby warship rescued the slavers and defeated the slaves. As punishment, Essjerrie's right hand was cut off, and he was hanged from the ship's mast. When he was dead, the crew threw his body into the ocean.

Enslaved Africans sometimes revolted on slave ships.

Escaping slavery

Instead of starting a rebellion, slaves could try to escape. Alone, an escaped slave usually didn't get very far before being caught. Joining a group of other escaped slaves, however, provided a better chance of freedom.

Runaway slaves hid in forests and swamps.

Maroon villages

Runaway slaves – called **maroons** – built villages deep in jungles, swamps, and mountains. In South America, some of these villages grew into small cities with more than 5,000 people. Maroons chose their own leaders and held on to their African traditions.

Maroons had to become good fighters in order to survive. First, they had to stay on the alert for slave hunters and soldiers sent to capture them. Second, they needed to raid plantations and colonial towns for tools and food. In Jamaica the maroon leader Cudjoe fought the British colonists from 1730 until 1740, when they finally agreed to give him and his followers a part of the island.

Beyond Africa

Despite endless work and harsh treatment, enslaved Africans built new lives in the Americas. In Africa each society had a unique language, music, religion, and social and legal system. In the Americas, slaves from these different societies blended their traditions and incorporated European traditions.

Slave religion

The religion of slaves is one example of the blending of the traditions. Many Africans kept their traditional religions. Some arrived as Muslims. Some were converted to Christianity. The owners often belittled African religious traditions, calling them "magic".

Slave families

Slaves considered their families important. The idea of family included a wide circle of people. Stolen from their African families, slaves thought of shipmates who made the **Middle Passage** with them as relatives. In the Americas, where owners could separate parents from their children, slaves treated neighbours and friends as family members.

Slave families were often split apart when one member was sold.

Buying freedom

A few slaves were allowed to earn money of their own and purchase themselves from their owners. But the law didn't give former slaves and other Africans living in the Americas the same rights as white colonists. In some places, they couldn't own land or attend school.

Some slaves did odd jobs in order to earn money to buy their freedom.

Venture Smith, a Free African

Venture Smith lived in the British **colonies** during the 1700s. Originally named Broteer, he was the son of a West African ruler. When he was eight years old, he was captured and sent to North America. Renamed "Venture Smith", he worked for several owners before he purchased his freedom in 1765 at the age of 36.

By cutting wood, growing watermelons, and fishing for lobsters, Smith gradually earned enough money to buy back his family: two sons, one daughter, and his wife Meg. Over the years, he also bought five other slaves in order to set them free. "My freedom," he said, "is a privilege which nothing else can equal."

Africans in Britain

Africans lived in Britain long before the beginning of the Atlantic slave trade. They first came as soldiers in the Roman army between 100 and 300 CE (Common Era). In the 700s, Muslim soldiers from North Africa conquered Spain and Portugal. Their descendants later spread across Europe.

Africans at the royal court

It is difficult to confirm how many Africans lived in Britain before the 1700s, but we do know that King Henry VIII had a black trumpeter in the 1500s. Royalty and the rich had black servants. In Scotland, according to the royal treasurer's records for the early 1500s, King James IV gave gifts to the Africans visiting his court.

Elizabeth I and the blackmoores

Queen Elizabeth I used black servants, but in 1596 she decided that England had too many blacks, or "blackmoores". In a letter to the mayor of London, she wrote, "There are of late divers blackmoores brought into this realme, of which kinde of people there are already here to manie." She ordered that they be sent out of the country. Elizabeth called on a merchant, Casper Van Senden, to round up blacks and take them to Spain and Portugal.

In 1601 Elizabeth complained about the black population again. She was angry that they were not Christian, "having no understanding of Christ or his Gospel". Elizabeth never succeeded in reducing the black population in England, but her words show that prejudice existed even in her time.

Slaves and free persons

More Africans arrived in Britain during the period of the slave trade. Those who came as slaves usually came with their owners from the colonies. African traders came on business, while children of African rulers came to study. Some Africans came as seamen on British merchant vessels.

Free Africans also lived in Britain. Many were servants, but some were farmers, **merchants**, shopkeepers, teachers, preachers, actors, sailors, or soldiers.

Soldiers and sailors

The British army in the Caribbean recruited free Africans and bought thousands of slaves to defend the colonies. In 1795 the army paid as much as £80 (more than £5,000 today) for an African who looked like a good soldier. All slaves in the British military were freed in 1807, but they were "free" in name only because they had to serve for life. White soldiers, in contrast, could leave the army after seven years. Often, they received higher pay and more promotions than African soldiers.

In Britain many Africans were servants of the rich.

Courage and loss

The slave trade deeply damaged African societies. Although many African rulers and traders profited, it brought war, hardship, and uncertainty. And the damage lasted long after the slave trade ended.

A valuable resource

The slave trade took one of Africa's most valuable resources – its people. Over a period of 420 years, millions of African men and women were sent to the Americas. These Africans were farmers, hunters, warriors, weavers, miners, judges, healers, and builders. They created art and music and invented new tools. They raised families. But slave owners claimed their work, their talent, and even their children.

Millions lost

How many Africans were enslaved? Traders did not keep good records, so historians can only try to estimate the number. Some historians say 50 million while others say 10 million. Today, 12 million seems the best estimate for the number of slaves taken from Africa to the Americas. Of these, at least one million died during the **Middle Passage**.

The slave trade robbed millions of Africans of their freedom and their families.

Personal loss

It is impossible to measure the human suffering caused by the slave trade. Enslaved Africans suffered disease and cruelty. They lost their homes and families. They were forbidden to use their own languages, practise their own religions, or even keep their own names. They had no rights at all because, according to the law, they were the property of their owners.

Hope

But the slave owners could not chain Africans' hearts and minds. There is a proverb from the Congo that says, "No matter how long the night, the day is sure to come." Africans clearly believed this. Men and women, both enslaved and free, fought bravely to win their freedom, stop the slave trade, and eventually end slavery.

This painting, *On to Liberty* by Theodor Kaufmann, shows hopeful slaves on their way to freedom.

Timeline

1443   Portuguese sailors reach the coast of West Africa.

1450s   Portuguese traders begin buying and selling slaves.

1482   The Portuguese build a fort at Elmina on the coast of West Africa.

1483   Portuguese explorers visit the Congo kingdom.

1488   The Portuguese explorer Bartolomeu Dias becomes the first European explorer to sail around the southern tip of Africa.

1492   Christopher Columbus arrives at the Americas.

1494   Portugal and Spain sign the Treaty of Tordesillas and divide the world between them.

1497–99

  Vasco da Gama, a Portuguese explorer, sails around Africa and across the Indian Ocean to southern India.

1505   The Portuguese attack and destroy Kilwa, a city on the east coast of Africa.

1506   Afonso I becomes King of the Congo.

1511   John Blanke, a trumpeter, takes part in a celebration given by King Henry VIII.

1518   Enslaved Africans are first taken directly from Africa to Spain's Caribbean colonies.

1526   The King of the Congo protests the slave trade.

1528–36

  The African Estevanico explores the region that later became the southwestern United States.

1542   Sir John Hawkins makes the first British slaving voyage between Africa and the Americas.

1550	The King of Benin outlaws the slave trade.
1607	Jamestown, the first successful British **colony** in North America, is founded.
1619	The first Africans arrive in Jamestown.
1627	The British start a colony on the Caribbean island of Barbados.
1637	The Dutch capture the West African settlement of Elmina from the Portuguese.
1641	The colony of Massachusetts makes slavery legal.
1655	The British start a colony on the Caribbean island of Jamaica.
1663	A Virginia court decides that if a slave woman has a baby, the baby is a slave too.
1672	King Charles II grants the Royal African Company control over British trade with Africa.
1713	Britain becomes a major player in the trans-Atlantic slave trade.
1738	The ship *Leusden* sinks. Instead of trying to rescue the slaves, the crew leaves them to drown.
1739	A slave named Jemmy leads the Stono Rebellion in South Carolina.
1750	Georgia becomes the last British colony in North America to make slavery legal.
1769	Essjerrie Ettin leads an unsuccessful slave **rebellion** on the ship *Guineese Vriendschap*.
1780	The King of Senegal outlaws the slave trade.

Glossary

brand owner's symbol burned on a slave or an animal

cargo goods carried by a ship

charter official document granting rights or privileges

civilize to become civil, or adequate, in a certain society

class group sharing the same status in a community. A community can have several different levels of classes.

colony distant territory under the control of another nation

conquistador Spanish soldier or adventurer

crew team of sailors on a ship

enterprise major undertaking, usually in business

indentured servant person who sells his or her labour for a certain amount of time

indigo plant used to make a dark blue dye for colouring cloth

malaria disease common in tropical areas; a cycle of fevers is one of the symptoms

maroon runaway slave

merchant business person who buys and sells goods

Middle East area of land between Africa and Asia

Middle Passage voyage carrying slaves across the Atlantic Ocean from Africa to the Americas

missionary person who tries to persuade others to adopt his or her religion

prisoner of war person captured by enemy soldiers

racism mistaken idea that a person's skin colour determines his or her worth as a human being

rebellion attempt to overthrow persons in power

smallpox contagious disease; small blisters are one of the symptoms

toll tax for using a road or bridge

treaty agreement between the rulers of different nations

tribute gift or payment to a ruler

yellow fever disease common in tropical areas

Find out more

Books

Africa: A Look Back, James Haskins and Kathleen Benson (Marshall Cavendish Benchmark, 2007)

The Atlantic Slave Trade, Don Nardo (Thomson/Gale, 2008)

The Slave Trade and the Middle Passage, S. Pearl Sharp and Virginia Schomp (Marshall Cavendish Benchmark, 2007)

Websites

History of slavery
www.understandingslavery.com/citizen/explore/historyofslavery/?page=1

Interactive map of the transatlantic slave trade
www.bbc.co.uk/history/british/abolition/map/index.shtml

National Archives, Black Presence: Asian and Black History in Britain, 1500–1850
www.nationalarchives.gov.uk/pathways/blackhistory/

Timeline of slavery
www.channel4.com/history/microsites/H/history/a-b/britains_slave_trade.html

Place to visit

International Slavery Museum
Albert Dock
Liverpool L3 4AQ
www.liverpoolmuseums.org.uk/ism

Index